naked in the kitchen

naked
in
the
kitchen

lynda martens

Naked in the Kitchen
first published 2010 by
Scirocco Drama
An imprint of J. Gordon Shillingford Publishing Inc.

Scirocco Drama Editor: Glenda MacFarlane
Cover design by Terry Gallagher/Doowah Design Inc.
Production photos by Ashley Athey
Author photo by Echo Gardiner
Printed and bound in Canada on 100% post-consumer recycled paper.

We acknowledge the financial support of the Manitoba Arts Council and The Canada Council for the Arts for our publishing program.

Production inquiries should be addressed to:
Angela Argento
Catalyst TCM Inc. Talent Creative Management
310 - 100 Broadview Avenue
Toronto, ON M4M 3H3
Ph. 416-645-0935 Fax 416-645-0936

Library and Archives Canada Cataloguing in Publication

Martens, Lynda
Naked in the kitchen / Lynda Martens.

A play.
ISBN 978-1-897289-56-3

I. Title.

PS8626.A76865N33 2010   C812'.6   C2010-903496-1

J. Gordon Shillingford Publishing
P.O. Box 86, RPO Corydon Avenue, Winnipeg, MB Canada R3M 3S3

In memory of my brother,
Michael Vanderloo (1966–1983).

Characters

Charlie Campbell: 45-60

Beth Campbell: 40-55

Michael Campbell: 18

Kevin: a friend of Michael's, 18

Production Notes

Although the play is set in rural Southwestern Ontario, it is acceptable for theatres using the script to alter the names of specific places and institutions of learning if so desired.

The play has a running time of near 90 minutes. Although the play is written without a formal intermisssion, a theatre using the script may have a strong preference for presenting it with an audience break in order to stretch legs or sell cookies. In that case, I would suggest that an appropriate place for an intermission might be on page 46, after Beth's line "Then why am I scared?" The second scene break (between scene two and three) should not be used as an intermission. This scene break is designed really as a scene in itself and the desired theatrical effect would be lost if an intermission was inserted here.

Production History

Naked in the Kitchen premiered at the Bloomington Playwrights Project, Bloomington, Indiana, on November 11, 2009, with the following cast:

MICHAEL Campbell .... Gabriel Wallace

CHARLIE Campbell .... Jeff Stone

BETH Campbell..Meredith Mills

KEVIN.. Kyle Hendricks

Director: Holly Holbrook

Set Design by Shane Cinal

Lighting Design by Travis Staley

Stage Manager: Josie Gingrich

Assistant Stage Manager: Shannon Walsh

Photographer: Natasha Komoda

Window Artist: Amber Zaragoza

Scenic Crew: Derrick Krober and Allie Goveia

Naked in the Kitchen started as a one-act play, and was first produced in that form at the London One Act Theatre Festival in June 2007. It then had a public reading in Nanaimo, BC with Theatre One, in their "Emerging Voices" program for promising playwrights in April 2008.

The first professional production of the one-act play was in Aurora, Ontario, as part of Theatre Aurora's Playwrights of Spring Festival, April, 2008, with the following cast:

BETH Campbell... Theresa Noon

CHARLIE Campbell .... David Tompa

Director: Michael Reinhart

Lighting and Sound Design by Benjamin Locke

Costume and Set Design by Maria Oltenau

Stage Manager: Karen Park

Assistant Stage Manager: Alexandra Skyler

Dramaturge: Ron Cameron-Lewis

It then benefitted from a reading with students at Fanshawe College, London, ON (leadership by John Dolan), and dramaturgical support from Dave Carley.

Playwright's Notes

The empty nest story plays out in hundreds of kitchens across the world every day. After twenty years of marriage and all the distractions that have filled the space between them from the rawness of intimacy, two parents send their child off into the world. It's a pivotal and terrifying time: "Wait…don't leave me alone *(with him/her)*!" "Do we have anything left to talk about?" "Do you still like me *(do I like you)*?" "Who *are* you *(who am I)*?" "Have you really been brushing your teeth that loudly all these years?" "I have work to do" "I need a drink."

The journey of *Naked in the Kitchen* has been simultaneous with my own rewarding and terrifying beginnings as a writer. It was 2006, when I first experienced a child moving away, that I started to record what I heard as Charlie and Beth's pressing dialogue in my mind. As a new playwright, I listened well to their voices back then because that was all I knew to do. As I have struggled to learn *how* to write and decipher what makes a play work (I hear the sound of playwrights laughing), I would sometimes impose my own will onto the page. Luckily, I have been constantly drawn or directed back to and led by the simple truth of these characters' voices. It is when I have listened most carefully that I have been best rewarded.

There are mixed emotions as I record personal notes about *Naked* going to press… "Is she ready?" "Have I done enough?" "But I'm not finished yet." There is excitement, yet I was perfectly happy rewriting…really, I was.

And there is trepidation as I send her out into the world. Will she find friends and be treated well? Will people understand her? And my precious Beth (who is some version of Me) …will they make her too angry or whiny? I surrender and trust.

For the solitary activity playwriting is, I have many people to thank. It truly takes a community, and many astonishing people and groups have contributed to the growth and development of this play.

Ron Cameron-Lewis was my first dramaturge, and his strong and gentle questions helped me deepen Charlie's character in the one-act play. Thank you Ron and the Playwrights of Spring Festival in Aurora for first bringing the one-act to its potential and for encouraging me to expand it into a full play.

Dave Carley was my mentor and dramaturge while he was playwright-in-residence at the London Public Library, 2008-2009. He saw me through several crucial drafts of the full play and always trusted me with what his "gut gut" feelings were. Thank you.

The Indiana-based Bloomington Playwright's Project, who chose the play as the winner of their 2009 Reva Shiner competition, worked with me through three months of rewrites and then gave the play a stunning three week run in their professional theatre. Holly Holbrook directed with an energetic and sensitive eye. I am eternally grateful for her transparency and courage in the process. Thanks also go to Richard Perez, Gabe Golden and Chad Rabinowitz for their input and wisdom. My Bloomington friends will always have a special place in my heart.

Thank you to Glenda MacFarlane and Gordon Shillingford at Scirocco Drama for their attention to detail and for believing in ths script.

The following people and groups also played a role in the jorney of this play: the London One-Act Festival, Paul Myers, Kevin Hassin, Rob Faust, Theatre One in Nanaimo, British Columbia, John Dolan and Fanshawe College students, and the DC Playwrights (Diane VanderHoven, Michael Wilmot, Richard Nagel, Terri Burman, Lucy Williams, Marion Johnson, Len Cuthbert and Dan Ebbs).

To my inspring and supportive family…Jerry, Lara, Justin, Lucas…thank you for tolerating my frequent disapperance into this alternate universe.

Lynda Martens

Lynda Martens is an actor/director/playwright from Granton, Ontario who has been writing since 2007. *Naked in the Kitchen* is her first script. Starting out as a one-act play, *Naked* attracted attention and won awards for its real characters and natural dialogue. In 2009, *Naked* was chosen by the Bloomington Playwrights Project as the winner of the Reva Shiner Playwrighting Competition. It received a development contract and a full production in Bloomington in November, 2009. Lynda has written other short plays, and is in the process of developing several full-length scripts. *Just For You* (one-act) was part of the 2009 Theatre Aurora's Playwrights of Spring Festival and The Bloor West Village Playhouse's Valentine weekend line-up in 2010. *Poison* (in development) is a dramatic look at family psychopathology on a rhubarb farm in rural Alberta. *Praying for Love* (in development) is a story about a priest forced to choose between a woman and his collar. Lynda's website is www.lyndamartens.com.

Scene One

The setting is a country kitchen in the Campbell home in a rural area near London, Ontario, Canada. There is a table with four chairs, and a cozy sitting area with a small couch. The furniture is slightly worn but comfortable, and the décor is warm, sunny and colourful. It is the morning that MICHAEL leaves for university. BETH and CHARLIE are present. CHARLIE is dressed casually but carefully. BETH is in lounge clothes or a bathrobe, and she has two large rollers in her hair that resemble Mickey Mouse ears. CHARLIE reads the paper and starts a crossword. BETH is busy in the kitchen.

BETH: More coffee?

CHARLIE: Hmmm?

BETH brings the coffee pot to him.

BETH: Coffee…?

CHARLIE: Sure.

BETH pours him more coffee.

CHARLIE: Thank you. *(Pause.)* We should be gone by ten-thirty. Any stirrings yet?

BETH: I thought we'd let him sleep a bit. *(Pause.)* Soy muffin?

Pause.

CHARLIE: Sure.

BETH: I know…they're a bit hard but we might as well eat them.

CHARLIE: Or we could…play hockey…?

Pause.

BETH: Your dad called. *(She hands CHARLIE a pink sticky note.)*

CHARLIE: And…

BETH: Something about helping him move some stuff—

CHARLIE: Shit!

BETH: What?

CHARLIE: I told him I'd get some things out of his shed today. Damn it! I completely forgot! *(Getting his phone and dialing.)*

BETH: It's not a big deal, Charlie. You can do it…

CHARLIE shushes BETH non-verbally.

(Whispering.) Tomorrow.

CHARLIE: Dad! Yeah, listen, I'm an idiot. I forgot we're driving Michael to Toronto today, so I *(Pause.)* … yeah…he's excited. *(Pause.)* OK. Tomorrow. Sure. See you then.

BETH: See?

CHARLIE: Beth…when you tell my father you're going to do something, you damn well better—

BETH: Oh he's fine. Bring him some soy muffins to make up for it.

CHARLIE: Yeah, that'll help.

BETH: He likes hockey.

Pause. BETH goes back to puttering, CHARLIE to his crossword.

CHARLIE: Vitamin prefix. Five letters…

Pause.

BETH: Ultra?

CHARLIE: Starts with "m".

Pause.

BETH: Multi?

CHARLIE: That works.

Long pause.

BETH: Hey…can I get you something to *eat*, Charlie?

CHARLIE: No thanks.

Pause.

BETH: What I mean is…can I get you something to *eat*, Charlie?

CHARLIE: I had a bagel.

Pause.

BETH: You've forgotten. *(Pause. CHARLIE looks confused.)* The code.

CHARLIE: What code?

Pause.

Oh. *That* code.

BETH: When I add a subtle *inflection* to the word *eat*—

CHARLIE: See, there's the glitch. I'm a guy, and guys don't get subtle inflections.

BETH: So I should spell it out…

CHARLIE: Maybe it's the hair. Will the rollers be in or out? Somebody could get hurt…

Pause. BETH throws a dish towel at CHARLIE, who yells up the stairs.

Michael! Time to get up!

BETH: Did you come to bed at all last night?

Pause.

CHARLIE: I was up late doing some paperwork and I guess I fell asleep in front of the TV.

BETH: It's happening a lot lately.

CHARLIE: A few times.

Pause. Sound of a toilet flushing.

BETH: Five.

CHARLIE: Sorry?

BETH: Five times in six weeks.

CHARLIE: You're counting?

BETH: That's more than a few.

CHARLIE: You're counting…

BETH: A few is three.

CHARLIE: So what's five? A horde? A throng?

BETH: A trend. Five is a trend.

CHARLIE: I can't believe you're keeping track.

BETH: It means I care, Charlie. Like you used to keep track of how often we made love, and when my period was due…

CHARLIE: I'm…stressed lately. Watching sports relaxes me.

BETH: We have a TV in our bedroom.

CHARLIE: With no satellite.

BETH: I miss your cold feet.

CHARLIE: I heard a flush. He's awake.

BETH: Fine.

CHARLIE: Fine.

BETH: Fine. *(Pause.)* Let's take him out for dinnner tonight.

CHARLIE: I'm sure he'd rather hang out with his new dorm mates.

BETH: One last steak dinner before he has to eat crap.

CHARLIE: I'm sure campus food has probably evolved in twenty years.

BETH: We'll let him decide.

MICHAEL enters during BETH's line. He clearly just rolled out of bed and is half asleep. He is wearing worn lounge pants and an old T-shirt. He has bed head. He is a laid-back teen but is a bit nervous today. He carries a hockey bag full of clothes, which he drops. He stretches and lets out a huge yawn.

CHARLIE: Hey! The big man on campus!

BETH: Morning sweetheart. *(She kisses him, sees the bag.)* Where's the rest?

MICHAEL: What?

BETH: I put the big suitcase in your room.

MICHAEL: I'm not moving to China, Mom.

BETH: OK…

Pause. MICHAEL plays with his mom's hair.

MICHAEL: I see she's channeling Mickey again.

BETH hugs MICHAEL. He hugs her back warmly.

BETH: Will you miss us?

MICHAEL: *(Mimicking Mickey.)* Oh gosh gee…I sure will!

BETH: Promise?

MICHAEL: Yes. *(They still hold each other.)*

CHARLIE: She's crying again, isn't she?

BETH: She is completely entitled to a few tears at this moment. You should try it sometime.

CHARLIE: I have no time for tears.

MICHAEL: Hey…no fighting in front of the child unit. *(MICHAEL looks in a cupboard.)*

BETH: How about pancakes?

MICHAEL: Do we have fresh bagels? *(MICHAEL starts to get some cold cereal out.)*

CHARLIE: In the freezer.

MICHAEL: No, Dad. There are no fresh bagels in the freezer. Fresh means unfrozen.

BETH: *(She looks in the freezer.)* I'll defrost some for you.

MICHAEL: Never mind. *(He pours milk onto the cereal and sits down to eat.)*

The buzz of a clothes dryer finishing a cycle is heard.

BETH: Bacon and eggs?

(l to r): Gabriel Wallace (Michael), Meredith Mills (Beth), and Jeff Stone (Charlie).

MICHAEL: I'm good.

BETH: Have a muffin.

She gives MICHAEL a muffin. BETH exits.

There is a non-verbal exchange between MICHAEL and CHARLIE regarding the hockey-puck muffin. There is silence. CHARLIE is still reading the paper and doing a crossword.

CHARLIE: Michael…five letters…respect or recognition…slang. Starts with 'p'.

Pause.

MICHAEL: Props?

CHARLIE: Thank you.

Pause. MICHAEL is moving something nervously…either twitching his leg up and down or tapping a spoon.

Nervous?

MICHAEL: Nope. *(MICHAEL continues the movement for a moment until CHARLIE calmly stops it with his hand.)* What?

CHARLIE: Nothing. *(Pause.)* That engineering program is a bitch.

MICHAEL: I guess. *(Pause.)* Listen, Dad, I know we've talked about this before, but…you started in engineering, right?

CHARLIE: Yes. My first year…

MICHAEL: So…what went wrong exactly?

CHARLIE: Nothing went wrong. It turned out that psychology was a better fit for me.

MICHAEL: OK...so when was it that you switched? I mean did—

CHARLIE: Oh!...Michael... *(He digs into a pocket.)* I forgot...I got some cash out for you, in case you're short.

MICHAEL: That's OK. I've got some saved up.

CHARLIE: I know. I just don't want you to be stressed about money. School will be hard enough. *(He hands him some cash.)*

MICHAEL: *(He takes the cash from CHARLIE.)* Sweet! Thanks.

BETH enters, carrying a basket of laundry.

BETH: *(Handing MICHAEL the basket.)* Socks... *(To CHARLIE.)* More coffee?

CHARLIE: No thanks.

BETH: What time are you supposed to be there? *(She gets a protein drink out of the fridge.)*

MICHAEL: Orientation starts at... *(He checks a paper on the table to be sure.)* one o'clock.

BETH: *(She hands MICHAEL the protein drink.)* We'll need to settle you in first.

MICHAEL: Ah...that stuff blows.

BETH: You need protein in the morning.

MICHAEL: But it's nasty.

BETH: Fine. Did you pack your vitamins? *(BETH drinks the protein herself.)*

MICHAEL: I won't take them anyway.

CHARLIE: Oh it's not about whether you take them or not, Michael. All you have to do is *pack* them, so your mom can feel less guilty.

BETH: Thank you Charlie. *(She takes a list out of her pocket and hands it to MICHAEL, who doesn't take it.)* Check this list.

MICHAEL: I have my own list.

BETH: Can I see it?

MICHAEL: It's...in my head.

Pause.

OK, OK... Jeans...dress pants?

BETH: Not jeans...no rips.

CHARLIE: Give him a second to wrap his head around the concept.

MICHAEL: *(Looking at the list again.)* T-shirts... Pajamas. These are fine.

BETH: They're old...and a little thin.

MICHAEL: Oh my God, Mom.

BETH: I bought you new ones.

MICHAEL: I don't need—

BETH: Please stop fighting me on everything, Michael. I can't make you breakfast, I can't buy you pajamas...I only have a few hours left to mother you so just let me do it.

MICHAEL: Fine.

CHARLIE: What's next on the list?

MICHAEL: Socks... What?! Holy shit... Mom!?

BETH: What?

MICHAEL: Unreal.

CHARLIE: What is it?

MICHAEL: Right after underwear *(Showing CHARLIE the list.)*.

CHARLIE: You spelled it wrong.

MICHAEL: Who cares?

BETH: I did not.

MICHAEL: Just cross it out.

CHARLIE: That should be an "n".

MICHAEL: I said—

BETH: That is an "n".

CHARLIE: It looks more like an "m".

BETH: *That's* an "m", and *that's* an "n".

MICHEAL: *(Snatching the list from CHARLIE.)* It doesn't matter. *(He rips up the list.)*

BETH: You'll need condoms.

MICHAEL: *(Loudly.)* What for?

Beat.

CHARLIE: Uh oh...

MICHAEL: I mean...I know what for, but...shit...I'll just get them when I need...shit...never mind.

BETH: Michael, we don't think you're very sexually active as yet, but—

MICHAEL: Oh my—

CHARLIE: Actually, I hadn't formed an opinion on the matter.

BETH: But I give it three weeks in that co-ed dorm before—

MICHAEL: Come on! Just because it's a co-ed dorm doesn't mean that everybody's…doing it all the time.

CHARLIE: Your mother's right. Dorm situations increase the likelihood that one will be…active.

MICHAEL: So…what? Now I can't stay in the dorm?

CHARLIE: We didn't say that. We've both lived in dormitories.

MICHAEL: Yeah, so—

CHARLIE: You will find very strange people there. My roommate used to bring girls into our room and… what's the word…bang? He'd bang them right in front of me.

BETH: Charlie!

MICHAEL: Dad…I—

CHARLIE: I didn't look. And girls can be just as forward. That was where your mother first threw herself at me.

BETH: Is that how you remember it?

MICHAEL: I really don't want to hear that story.

BETH: So when was the last time you used a condom?

CHARLIE: Don't answer that.

BETH has gone to a drawer and gets a box of condoms; gives them to MICHAEL.

BETH: We'll practice.

MICHAEL: Oh no no no…we are *not* practicing. *(He puts the package down.)*

BETH: Relax…you can use a banana. *(Grabbing a banana from the fruit bowl and giving it to MICHAEL.)* Sit down.

MICHAEL: This is nuts.

CHARLIE: *(Picking up the package.)* Combo pack!

BETH: *(To CHARLIE.)* I couldn't decide between the lubricated, ribbed, or flavoured ones. And it seems to be one size fits all until you get up to extra large, but I didn't think he—

MICHAEL: Stop! *(He starts to walk out.)* I am so outa here.

CHARLIE: Michael!

BETH stops MICHAEL as CHARLIE takes the box, opens it and takes out a packaged condom and hands it to MICHAEL.

BETH: We need to know that you can do this.

CHARLIE: It might save you some fumbling around in the dark.

BETH: Just put the banana between your knees, and… Charlie, you're the father. You help him.

MICHAEL: I don't need help.

CHARLIE: I'll spot you from here.

BETH: Open the package.

MICHAEL goes to use his teeth.

Not with your teeth.

MICHAEL: This is so…wrong.

BETH: Your father will read the instructions. I won't watch.

CHARLIE: Do you have it with the roll-side—

MICHAEL: YES!

CHARLIE: Good, now…slide the condom down the erect… *(CHARLIE starts laughing.)* banana…I'm sorry.

MICHAEL quickly rolls the condom down the banana.

MICHAEL: I hope you both enjoyed humiliating me.

BETH: Michael, more than half of college students who are sexually active contract a disease. And some of those STDs aren't even stopped by a condom.

MICHAEL: Mom…just…

CHARLIE: I think your mother is saying that you have to take responsibility for your own… *(CHARLIE slowly pushes a tissue box across the table to MICHAEL.)* needs.

Pause.

MICHAEL: Are you kidding me?

BETH: Sweetheart, I clean your room.

MICHAEL: Look, this was a trip, folks, but I'm done. *(He goes to throw out the banana.)*

BETH: *(BETH stops him.)* That is a perfectly good banana.

MICHAEL: My parents are freaks. *(MICHAEL exits.)*

Pause.

CHARLIE: We are cruel.

BETH: Better safe than sorry. *(Pause.)* Hey, I found the Disney picture the other day; Michael with Mickey. Let's sneak it in his bag.

CHARLIE: He finally had hair.

BETH: I was so glad to be rid of that stupid dirty ball cap… *(Pause.)* It's almost three years.

CHARLIE: I know.

BETH: Oh…I just remembered… Michael has a follow-up appointment with Dr. Cholmski this month. Where did I write that down? *(Looking for the paper.)* I think it was the twenty-first… I know I put it in this drawer. Did you see it?

CHARLIE: No I didn't.

BETH: It was on one of those little pink pieces of paper.

CHARLIE: Those things are everywhere, Beth. Do you realize how much time you waste looking for those pink sticky notes?

BETH: I don't need a lecture right now, Charlie. Help me look.

CHARLIE: OK. Where should I start?

BETH: Anywhere. *(She's starting to get upset, looking everywhere.)* I know I wrote it down by the phone.

CHARLIE: *(CHARLIE starts looking and is finding sticky notes.)* What's written on it?

BETH: If I knew that, I wouldn't need to find the paper! Why is nothing where I put it?

CHARLIE: You can always call the hospital and find out when—

BETH: I probably threw it out by accident. Wait… *(Finding one. Reading.)* September twenty-fifth, ten o'clock. *(It's the wrong paper.)* No, I know I put Dr. Cholmski's name on it. And this is your handwriting. *(She puts it back in the drawer and moves to look somewhere else.)*

CHARLIE: *(CHARLIE goes to the drawer. He retrieves the paper BETH read and puts it in his pocket.)* Why don't I just call the hospital?

BETH: Who keeps throwing those papers away? Somebody must have seen it.

CHARLIE: Actually, yes, there's a whole conspiracy going on, Beth. We hide those little pink papers all over the house just to drive you crazy.

BETH: Funny isn't helping right now.

CHARLIE: Panicking isn't helping either.

BETH: Look, Charlie!

CHARLIE: I'm looking. We've got time, Beth.

BETH: He's leaving today. We need it now! *(BETH is in tears now.)*

CHARLIE: It's just a piece of paper. *(He goes to her, softly.)* Hey…

Pause.

BETH: I'm not ready Charlie. It's too soon.

CHARLIE: I know.

BETH: Can we lock him up?

CHARLIE: It's against the law.

BETH: Just one more year. That's all I want.

CHARLIE: We can't hold him back, Beth. He's ready.

BETH: But I'm not. God, how can you be so calm?

CHARLIE: Children grow up.

BETH: This is our only baby. We almost lost him and that

was like yesterday, and who's going to take care of him out there?

CHARLIE: He's still close. *(Pause.)* And he'll be fine.

BETH: You don't know that.

Pause.

I think we should have a party soon…for the three year mark.

CHARLIE: Sure.

Pause.

BETH: It's getting late. I should go make myself presentable.

BETH exits. CHARLIE finishes his coffee and cleans up MICHAEL's cereal bowl and whatever else is left out.

MICHAEL enters. He opens his gym bag and starts putting the socks inside.

CHARLIE: You're recovered?

MICHAEL: Ah…no. *(Pause.)* Listen…can we talk?

CHARLIE: Sure. Hey, how about we have dinner together after we settle you in.

MICHAEL: Really?

CHARLIE: Your mom's idea. I told her you'd probably rather be making some new friends, but…

MICHAEL: Where would we go?

CHARLIE: Steak?

MICHAEL: Can we decide later?

CHARLIE: Of course. *(Pause.)* We're taking your desk, right?

MICHAEL: Yeah…and the futon…and the small dresser.

CHARLIE: I hope it all fits in the truck. *(He goes to leave.)*

MICHAEL: *(About to tell CHARLIE something.)* Hey… Dad?

CHARLIE: Yes?

Pause.

MICHAEL: Listen, um…there's something I should…you know we were… *(He chickens out.)* …there's a couple of books…beside my bed I should bring. Can you grab them?

CHARLIE: Sure thing.

MICHAEL: Thanks.

CHARLIE exits.

(To himself.) Chickenshit…

Music fades in as MICHAEL stands for a moment and then exits. Fadeout.

Scene Two

Later that same day, around three o'clock. CHARLIE and BETH have returned home from delivering MICHAEL to his dorm at the University of Toronto. CHARLIE enters, gets out his laptop and sits with it at the table, starting to work. He might also have a cellphone that he attends to periodically. He is distant and focused on his work. BETH enters, carrying a laundry basket.

BETH: Do you want a sandwich?

CHARLIE: What?

BETH: *(Patiently.)* Do you want a sandwich?

CHARLIE: Oh, sure…uh…have we got any of that…um…

BETH: No, we're out of that…there's the other stuff though…with the garlic…you had it last week. *(Pause.)* You liked it.

CHARLIE: OK. Thanks.

BETH: *(During this segment BETH puts the laundry basket down, gathers the sandwich ingredients, places them on the table and makes the sandwich at the table. CHARLIE keeps his eyes on his laptop.)* I have to go to town tomorrow so I'll pick up some of that turkey you like. *(Pause.)* I've been thinking. I might go up and see Mom at the cottage next weekend. She's been asking me to come. I think she's lonely. *(Pause.)* And while I'm up there I might just stay…and hang out at the lake for a few days *(Notices that CHARLIE is not listening.)* …at the lake. I've always loved September at the lake. All those noisy summer people are gone. With Michael away, it'll be nice that we can take off and do things like that more. *(Pause.)* Do you want to join me? *(She again notices he is not listening.)* OK. Actually, I think I'll go alone, and while I'm up there I might just see if that cute neighbour Roger is up for a quick roll in the sack. *(She plunks the sandwich on the table.)*

CHARLIE: What? Oh, thanks.

Pause. BETH hands CHARLIE a glass of water.

BETH: A toast…to official empty nesters.

CHARLIE: *(Without looking up.)* Empty nesters…

BETH: Just the two of us…for now, anyway.

CHARLIE: What do you mean?

BETH: *(BETH starts to clear the sandwich materials off the table.)* Oh I don't know. My friends keep telling me how kids these days move out, then when school's done or when they need money…well apparently they come back.

CHARLIE: Not if you change the locks, they don't.

BETH: It's just wishful thinking. *(Beat.)* He looked almost eager to be rid of us today, actually.

CHARLIE: Parents have no place in a dormitory.

BETH: He seemed OK, didn't he? It looked like he had picked out a few potential friends already.

CHARLIE: Michael is a very social young man. You worry far too much about him.

BETH: But he gets anxious sometimes. I would feel better if he was closer. I keep thinking we should have looked more closely at Western's programs. He could have lived at home.

CHARLIE: I think that was precisely why he chose U. of T., dear.

Pause.

BETH: Are you going to miss him?

CHARLIE: What?

BETH: Are you going to miss him?

CHARLIE: Why would you ask that?

BETH: It's just a question. You were so…quiet and moody all the way home and you don't talk about him leaving and…I don't know; it was just a question.

CHARLIE: Well it's a dumb question, Beth. He's my son; of course I'll miss him but I'll wait for the tires on the truck to cool first, would that be alright? You're obsessing. *(Pause. BETH has poured herself a glass of wine.)* Beth.

BETH: Yes?

CHARLIE: It's three o'clock.

BETH: So?

CHARLIE: Nothing.

BETH: *(Playfully upset.)* Oh never mind me. I'm just dumb and what was that other word you used? Obsessive…right. Now I'll be dumb, obsessive and drunk too! It's quite comforting to have an identity. I'll have to remind myself of that whenever I get confused and forget who I am. It's OK Beth, calm down, don't panic. Remember? You're the dumb obsessive drunk!

CHARLIE: Beth, I didn't say you were…let's just forget it, alright?

BETH: No name calling.

CHARLIE: I didn't call you a name. I said it was a dumb *question.*

BETH: Oh…

CHARLIE: And, OK, I may have called you obsessive. No… no I didn't. I said you were *obsessing*. That's a *verb,* not an adjective. And I certainly did not call you a drunk. What I did was state the time of day. I merely said it was three o'clock.

BETH: There you go getting all symantical again. Sometimes the tone and meaning of what you say matters more than the actual words, my dear.

CHARLIE: Symantical isn't even a word, Beth. See? I'm typing in 'symantical'…and look…spell-check puts a little red line under it that tells me that it's not… *(Pause.)* Beth…look, I'm just teasing you.

BETH: Not now.

CHARLIE: Ahhh…jeez… I'm sorry. Let's please just forget it, alright? You're upset because Michael's gone.

BETH: Shouldn't I be? Don't you feel this big…hole? It's like, logically… in my head, I want him to live his life…I know he has to go. I know he hasn't *left me*. But why I feel so *abandoned*?

CHARLIE: Maybe you *should* go to your mother's cottage for the weekend. It would give you a chance to relax, and—

BETH: I'm gonna call him. *(She goes to get the phone.)*

CHARLIE: Beth…

BETH: To see if he needs anything.

CHARLIE: *(Stopping her.)* We can't call him. It's in the parents' rulebook.

Pause. CHARLIE returns to his computer.

BETH: Why do you always have to be right?

CHARLIE: You used to like it.

BETH: Did I?

CHARLIE: Mm hm.

BETH: Well it's a quality that is considerably less attractive after twenty years.

CHARLIE: I'll try to be wrong more often.

BETH: Thank you.

Pause. BETH continues cleaning and CHARLIE is engaged with his laptop.

BETH: Come to the lake with me.

CHARLIE: What?

Beat. BETH chuckles.

BETH: Will you come to the lake with me?

CHARLIE: *(CHARLIE is looking at his computer.)* Let's see… definitely not if you're going to be boinking the neighbour the whole time we're there. What's his name? Roger something-or-other?

BETH: You…I *will* go to the lake alone and you can stay here and make love to your laptop. And maybe I will look up old Roger.

CHARLIE: Roger Dodger…

BETH: You don't think I would…

CHARLIE: I am not afraid to call your bluff…no.

BETH: You're no fun. *(Pause.)* I don't even know if his name is Roger. But he is cute, and he has been giving me the eye.

CHARLIE: Seriously, Beth…if you want to go, go. I couldn't stop you, and I trust you—

BETH: OK…I lied. He's really hairy. Not good hairy either…it's a…caveman kind of hairy.

CHARLIE: Too bad. While you were out with Roger I could have had a few adventures of my own…

BETH: Oh with who? Little Joanie Webster down at the restaurant? *(Mimicking, exaggerated.)* Would you like some extra whipped cream on your rice pudding, Mr. Campbell?

CHARLIE: She does not—

BETH: Let's go together, Charlie. No laptop, no TV, just you and me and the waves and the sunsets…

CHARLIE: And your mother.

BETH: We could always lock her in her room. *(Pause.)* My mother is fine. We'll have lots of time alone together.

CHARLIE: Hmmmm…

BETH: Are you even listening? This is crazy. I can't even get eye contact with you and I'm still excited at the thought of us being alone together.

CHARLIE: You can't help it. I'm adorable.

Pause.

BETH: Wait. What am I talking about? *(BETH thinks for a minute, takes a few gulps of her wine and seductively clears the table except for the laptop during this segment. She may also put some music on or hum a song as she clears the table.)* We don't have to go to any cottage to be alone together. Do you see anybody else here? *(She opens a cupboard or two.)* Anybody hiding in there? Nope… *(Beat.)* I think it's just you and me baby.

CHARLIE: I have work to do.

BETH: You know, I do believe that I once heard…that if you work too much your sexual organs start to… atrophy. *(Pause.)* Oooh, I used a big word!

CHARLIE: You heard that, did you?

BETH: I did. I read it in a magazine.

CHARLIE: Interesting study. But they forgot to factor in that I have a report to finish.

BETH: Report later. Play now. *(She picks up the laptop.)*

CHARLIE: Beth…

BETH: Just a little teeny break. Then you can get back to this.

CHARLIE: OK OK…just…let me save it first.

BETH: Fine. *(He does that and she snaps the laptop shut and puts it on a chair.)* Now, where were we? *(Pause.)* I know… let's play pretend…like we used to. You … you can be Roger, and I'll be a beautiful mermaid who comes swimming up to the shore of Lake Huron and says—

CHARLIE: Lake Huron doesn't have mermaids.

BETH: God you're boring. *(Pause.)* Hey this table's still pretty sturdy. I bet it could take some rockin'. *(She sits on the table and rocks back and forth to see if the table is sturdy.)*

CHARLIE: Beth, you're going to… *(Pause. BETH gives him a look and a gasp.)* strain…strain the table. I didn't say—

BETH: Break. You were going to say break!

CHARLIE: No, I wasn't. You said it. I didn't.

BETH: That's OK. I know I look good. Don't I look good, baby? *(She rocks some more.)*

CHARLIE: Yes. But please stop shaking the table.

BETH: Oh Charlie, loosen up…cool off…chillax… *(Beat.)* Sometimes…I think you came out of your mother's womb with a teeny weenie little seatbelt on. *(Pause.)* Come here. Mmmm… you always smell so good… without cologne or anything…just you. *(Pause.)* Do you know how long it's been since we made love on this table?

CHARLIE: Since we could afford a bed?

BETH: All our sexy adventures were pre-Michael. Now, we can do it wherever… and whenever we want!

CHARLIE: Theoretically speaking.

BETH: You know…there may be some real benefits to not having a child around the house anymore.

CHARLIE: Lower grocery bills…some peace and quiet…

BETH: No, Charlie. Not quiet. Noise! We can make *noise*! No more worrying about waking Michael up, or him and his friends watching TV in the next room. And I won't have to hold on to the headboard anymore to keep it from squeaking. You burn extra calories when you scream. *(Pause.)* Come on. Tell me you haven't wanted more screaming.

CHARLIE: I…

BETH: Don't all men want more screaming?

CHARLIE: I don't know.

BETH: Aaaand, we can even walk around the house… naked!

Pause. CHARLIE is getting aroused by BETH's touching. They kiss passionately for a moment and heat things up. BETH puts her hands on CHARLIE's buttocks, and that's when CHARLIE decides enough is enough.

CHARLIE: Beth… We have windows, and nosy neighbours.

BETH: Let them watch! *(She reaches for his belt and unbuckles it.)*

CHARLIE: Stop!

BETH: Why?

CHARLIE: Oh God, Beth, I really do want to, but…can we do this later?

BETH: Screw later!

CHARLIE: Yes…screw…later.

BETH: We'll be quick. Right here on this kitchen table. *(Removes crumbs from the table with her hands.)* I'll even wash it first if you want…I know how you like things clean. *(She licks her finger and scrubs a sticky spot off, and lies down on the table in a super sexy pose.)* Come on baby. Take me.

CHARLIE: I want to…really. But I can't. *(Pause.)* I'm sorry. *(He moves away.)*

Pause.

BETH: Well…it's your loss buddy boy, because the whole mood is long gone now. And you never know when I'll be able to get this old booty fired up again. *(Pause.)* It's been almost two months.

CHARLIE: Marriages have ups and downs. It's perfectly normal.

BETH: Screw normal. I want what we had. Do you know what they call a marriage with no sex? I heard this on Oprah the other day…they call it an anorexic marriage; a skinny, unfed, starving, pathetic, dying, anorexic marriage.

CHARLIE: Well praise be to Oprah! …If Oprah said it…then it must be true!

BETH: Charlie, be serious. *(Pause.)* I miss you.

CHARLIE: You're being melodramatic. I'm right here…

BETH: *(Pouring another glass of wine.)* Maybe we just don't have much to talk about anymore. *(Beat.)* Do you realize we could still have *forty more years* together?

CHARLIE: You say that like it's a bad thing…

BETH: Forty years!

CHARLIE: We don't know what we have Beth.

BETH: What the hell are we going to talk about?!

CHARLIE: *(Returning to the table and setting up the laptop again.)* Arthritis...constipation... hemorrhoids.

BETH: Speak for yourself.

CHARLIE: The unruliness of the younger generation...

BETH: Charlie I mean it. What are we going to—

CHARLIE: *Look maybe I don't want to talk!*

Pause.

BETH: Oh.

Long pause. The room gets a little chilly. CHARLIE decides to raise a white flag.

CHARLIE: I'm not playing board games with your mother.

BETH: *(BETH takes this to mean he'll come to the lake.)* No board games. We could bring a blanket out to our secret spot.

CHARLIE: Beth...

BETH: And be very quiet.

CHARLIE: Beth...not now.

BETH: OK. No pressure. *(BETH walks away to pick up a laundry basket and dumps the laundry on the table to fold it.)* We can talk about the lurid details later. *(She is folding laundry and is sorting underwear...sees that CHARLIE is giving her a look.)* What?

CHARLIE: Nothing.

BETH: OK. *(She continues folding and notices CHARLIE looking again.)* What?

CHARLIE: Nothing.

Pause. CHARLIE has the look on his face again.

BETH: What? That is the same look you've been giving me for weeks now.

Pause.

CHARLIE: Beth…*(Pause.)* There's something I…

Pause.

BETH: What is it?

Pause.

CHARLIE: You're folding underwear on the table.

Pause.

BETH: So…?

CHARLIE: It bugs me. That's it, that's all…end of story.

BETH: I always fold underwear on the table.

CHARLIE: Yes, well…we also *eat* on the table.

BETH: Its clean underwear, Charlie.

CHARLIE: I know that.

BETH: How did I not know this until now?

CHARLIE: Because it's not a big deal. Let's drop it please.

BETH: *(Playing with a thong.)* So…do you mean because this little stringy part here goes in my…and this wider part here goes between my legs and gets… *mmme…* on it? That's why you don't want this dirty little thing anywhere near the altar where you eat your food?

CHARLIE: You are making way too much of this.

BETH: You are afraid of my underwear!

CHARLIE: No. I am not afraid of your underwear.

BETH: Prove it.

CHARLIE: Fine. *(CHARLIE puts the thong in his mouth for a moment and pulls it out.)* Happy now?

BETH: Yes.

CHARLIE: This is exactly why I don't tell you things, you know. Everything's a huge...production.

BETH: Oh lighten up Charlie. If it bugs you, I will fold the underwear elsewhere. *(Beat.)* It does explain why you don't want to ravage me on the kitchen table. *(Pause.)* Awww, I shouldn't make fun of your little phobia.

CHARLIE: It's not a phobia. And I really don't—

BETH: Wait! Was there a...you know...an *incident* when you were young...like a trauma? Maybe you witnessed something! That's how these things start isn't it?

CHARLIE: Beth, you're being ridiculous.

BETH: Come on...You're the psychologist. Maybe...one night on the farm, you go out to the barn after dinner to do chores, and you come back...a little early...and walk right in on your parents going at it like dogs on the kitchen table...

CHARLIE: Can you stop?

BETH: ...with the leftover chicken still sitting there and it leaves you with this crazy hang up about sex and food and—

CHARLIE: I do not have any hang-ups! And my parents certainly did not EVER have... Oh God, thanks for that visual.

BETH: I'm just fooling around, Charlie.

(l to r): Meredith Mills (Beth) and Jeff Stone (Charlie).

CHARLIE: Well, don't! Because I'm...not fooling around, alright? I don't like being laughed at when I'm trying to tell you something important.

BETH: Oh. *(Pause.)* I'm sorry. The whole underwear thing didn't seem so important to me, I guess.

CHARLIE: Well...it is.

BETH: OK, so... *(Pause.)* Do you need to talk more about the underwear thing?

CHARLIE: No. I don't. It's not a big deal. I just really wish you wouldn't have to make such a big deal out of everything.

Pause.

BETH: I don't think I make a big deal out of *everything*.

CHARLIE: No...you don't. Never mind.

BETH: And I'm a bit confused at this point. It's important... the underwear thing, but it's not a big deal. Is that right?

CHARLIE: Could you stop saying that please?

BETH: What am I saying?

CHARLIE: Underwear thing. You keep calling it the underwear thing.

BETH: Well what am I supposed to call it?

CHARLIE: You don't understand.

BETH: But I'm trying to, Charlie. I want to understand you.

Pause.

CHARLIE: I want that too. *(Pause. He looks her in the eye. It's a different look.)*

Long pause.

BETH: This isn't about the underwear…is it?

Pause.

CHARLIE: No.

Pause.

BETH: It never was…was it?

Pause.

CHARLIE: No.

Pause.

BETH: So…you're OK with my thongs on the—

CHARLIE: Yes. I'm fine with your…off, on…clean, dirty… yes.

Pause.

BETH: Is something wrong? *(Pause. She looks at his face carefully.)* Oh.

CHARLIE: What?

BETH: I'm right. I was hoping to be wrong.

CHARLIE: Beth, I…don't know how to do this.

Pause.

BETH: Is it…is there someone else?

CHARLIE: What? No! God! No, Beth. God…I'm not…I'm not having an affair.

BETH: Are you sure?

CHARLIE: I think I'd know.

BETH: OK. Then what's happening?

CHARLIE: It's not a big deal.

BETH: Then why am I scared?

CHARLIE: Sit down.

She sits.

You won't get upset?

BETH: Charlie…

CHARLIE: You will, won't you?

BETH: Well I can't promise that, can I? I mean, that depends on what it is. *(Pause. CHARLIE is silent.)* Charlie…we have made it through…the worst.

Pause.

CHARLIE: Last month…when I said I was in Texas for that conference…

Pause.

BETH: You weren't in Texas

CHARLIE: No. I was in the hospital. I had surgery.

BETH: Surgery?

CHARLIE: Yes.

BETH: Charlie…? What are you—

CHARLIE: It's alright. I know this must feel like a shock to you, but I can—

BETH: What kind of surgery?

CHARLIE: I had something removed. A very small…lump.

BETH: A lump. Where?

Pause.

CHARLIE: In my scrotum.

BETH: What?! Oh my God… Charlie. Are you OK?

CHARLIE: I'm fine.

BETH: Oh baby! I can't believe you're telling me this. Are you alright? Are you in pain? What happened?

CHARLIE: It's going to be fine.

BETH: Don't...sugar coat. I don't understand. This happened…when did you say?

CHARLIE: I found the lump in July.

BETH: July? Charlie…

CHARLIE: Yes.

Pause.

BETH: So they…did a biopsy?

CHARLIE: Yes.

BETH: And…?

CHARLIE: It'll be alright, Beth…it doesn't matter…

BETH: How can you say that? You know it matters!

CHARLIE: No. The doctors said they probably got it all…

BETH: Tell me! Yes…or no *(Pause.)* It was…wasn't it?

CHARLIE: Yes, but—

BETH: I can't breathe.

CHARLIE: They took out some lymph nodes from my abdomen so they could be sure it hadn't spread. *(He laughs.)* It was pretty cool, actually. They sent this little tiny video camera right into my abdomen, and—

BETH: Do you really think I care about the technology? Charlie, I care about you! Has it spread?

Pause.

Has it?

CHARLIE: They don't know yet.

BETH: When will they know?

CHARLIE: I have an appointment on the twenty-fifth.

Pause.

BETH: The pink paper… *(BETH remembers and goes to get the pink slip of paper in the drawer.)* Where is it?

CHARLIE: Beth, listen…it's Spermatocytic Seminoma and they said they're optimistic.

BETH: I'm not sure it makes a difference whether your physician is an optimist or not, Charlie. *(Pause.)* I don't understand. Why didn't you tell me? I should have been there with you. Why wasn't I there? *(Pause.)* Why didn't you want me there with you?

CHARLIE: I did want you there with me. I'm sorry… I didn't want to upset you, and—

BETH: But how can I not be upset when something like this is happening to you? *(Pause. BETH is half talking to herself, in a bit of a dazed, dissociated state.)* It makes no sense. Husbands don't do this. No…husbands say to their wives, "Honey, I haven't been feeling right for a while." Wait. No, no, no no… That's wrong. They don't say that. They say *(Pause.)* … nothing. They don't say anything. No, they just walk around in pain, and their *wives* say, "Honey, are you alright?", and the husbands say, "Oh, it's nothing." *(She is slowly pulling magnets off the fridge and dropping them to the ground.)* But their wives are good, observant wives, and they know something is wrong. And then there are months and months of wives saying, "I think we better get you to the doctor", and husbands in complete denial, but—

CHARLIE: Beth, honey…

BETH: But their wives insist, and there's—

CHARLIE: Beth… *(He tries to touch her but she pushes him away.)*

BETH: There's this whole conversation that happens for months or years. We know that men don't go to the doctor on their own, because they're too strong and stubborn…*(Pause.)* or scared maybe…I don't know. But that's what they do! That's why men *need wives* Charlie…

CHARLIE: I know…

BETH: To listen to them and know them, and take care of them and take them to the stupid doctor!

CHARLIE: I know. I'm sorry.

BETH: Baby, you're sick and I didn't even notice. What kind of wife am I? I was supposed to be there with you! That's my job!

CHARLIE: Oh God, Beth, it all happened so fast. I tried to say it so many times…

BETH: But why didn't you?

CHARLIE: I thought I would go in and they would remove the lump and everything would be over.

BETH: That makes no sense.

CHARLIE: Getting Michael ready for school…you were both so happy, and I couldn't spoil that for you, or for Michael. I thought if I just took care of it first—

BETH: But you're sick. You needed me.

CHARLIE: *(Almost to himself.)* I'm not sick. I'm not sick. I'm sorry.

BETH: Stop apologizing. It is so hard to be angry with you when you're always saying you're sorry.

CHARLIE: I know. I'm sorry.

Pause.

They had to remove one of my testicles.

BETH: What? Oh my God, Charlie! *(Pause.)* Oh baby, you must be in pain…

CHARLIE: I'm fine.

Pause.

BETH: You're fine *(Pause.)* You've been walking around the house for five weeks…with a missing testicle?

CHARLIE: Yes.

Pause.

BETH: This is why we haven't been making love.

CHARLIE: Yes. But, Beth, I'm fine. Really.

BETH: Oh Charlie, you just don't get it…do you? *(Pause.)* The problem is not just the…lump. The problem… is that this horrible thing happened to you, and you came home and looked at my face day after day after day and somehow decided not to share this with me…with your wife. And now…and this is the stupidest part, because…I'm supposed to be… comforting you right now. I know that, but I can't… make myself. I can't. I'm so angry with you.

CHARLIE: I wanted to fix it first.

BETH: But, if it was good news on the twenty-fifth, would you ever have told me?

CHARLIE: Of course I would.

Pause.

BETH: Wait. You would have had to eventually, right?

CHARLIE: Yes.

BETH: Because I would see you. You'd be walking out of the shower one day and forget to hide yourself, or the towel would slip, and I'd see you naked, and I'd casually say, "Excuse me, Charlie, but…what happened to your other ball?"

CHARLIE: Beth, I…

BETH: I was pretty sure you used to have two of them.

CHARLIE: Could you stop?

BETH: Or maybe you were planning to get a prosthetic? Then you'd never have to tell me at all.

CHARLIE: I should have looked into it.

BETH: Do they even do that?

CHARLIE: I have no idea.

BETH: You must have been terrified that I would touch you…

CHARLIE: It's OK. *(Beat.)* You didn't.

Pause.

BETH: Why does this keep happening to us?

CHARLIE: Beth, please don't be upset. It'll be OK.

BETH: That was always your solution with Michael. "It's going to be OK, Beth"…"He's going to be fine"…

CHARLIE: Beth, don't…

BETH: Where's the laptop… *(Going to the laptop.)* What did you say? Sperma…what?

CHARLIE: Beth…

BETH: It's OK. It'll be our project. We will fight this together like we did—

CHARLIE: No! Beth, stop!

BETH: Why?

CHARLIE: *(Firmly.)* Listen to me. I want to be in charge of this. It's about me.

BETH: It is not just about you.

CHARLIE: I know. That's not what I meant, but I need to handle this.

BETH: What are you talking about? We have to do this together. You can't just keep shutting me out.

Pause.

CHARLIE: OK, let me say it a different way. *(Pause.)* Sometimes…you let things consume you. When Michael was sick, you stopped working. You've never gone back to nursing.

BETH: He needed me.

CHARLIE: He hasn't for a while. And my worry…my worry is that, with Michael gone, you're going to focus every ounce of your energy on me, and my…problem.

BETH: I don't understand.

CHARLIE: I don't want to be your project.

BETH: Our project. I was talking about "us", not "me". I don't want to take over; I want to be with you.

CHARLIE: It *feels* like you're taking over. *(Pause.)* With Michael, you took over.

Pause.

BETH: Michael… When Michael was sick, I couldn't work. I couldn't think about anything else. My son was sick!

CHARLIE: Our son.

BETH: He needed me! And why are you bringing him into this? This isn't about Michael.

Pause.

CHARLIE: You had to be the one to take him to all his appointments. You controlled every moment; what he ate, what he watched on television, all the diets and vitamins, chasing every alternative healer within a thousand mile radius. It consumed you completely.

BETH: And what would you have had me do, Charlie…let him die?

CHARLIE: You could have let him breathe. And you could have let me help…

BETH: What? Oh no, you don't…you've got it backwards, mister. *(Pause.)* You left me alone! You went off to hide at work and at your computer and you left me with all that shit to take care of! That kid needed somebody, and I was the only one there.

CHARLIE: I had to work. Somebody did. *(Pause.)* And you didn't seem to need me for anything.

Pause.

BETH: You think I didn't need you?

CHARLIE: That's what it felt like.

BETH: *(Crying, softer here but not able to approach him.)* Oh, God…this makes no sense. Not need you? *(Pause.)* I needed you so badly, Charlie. More than I could ever describe. So many times I wanted to just come home and do nothing but fall into your arms.

CHARLIE: Why didn't you?

BETH: You weren't there. And when you were...I don't know...you never acted like you wanted to be near any of it. You were working late every night. When he was vomiting his guts out after a treatment... where were you? When I cried myself to sleep night after night, where were you?

CHARLIE: There was no room for me.

BETH: No room for you?! Goddamn it, Charlie, grow up! I'm not your mother and it wasn't my job to take care of you. There was no time for either of us to think of anything but our son. If you needed something, then you should have fought for it like the rest of us.

CHARLIE: What I needed was for you to...

BETH: Stop it. You sound like your father...always blaming someone else.

Pause.

CHARLIE: This isn't getting us anywhere. I've said what I needed to say. This is my problem. I'll handle it. It will be fine.

BETH: Fine.

CHARLIE: Fine.

BETH: Fine. I'll just go get myself a life of my own then and you can take care of yourself from now on, since you don't need me for anything. *(Pause.)*

CHARLIE: Fine.

BETH starts to clean the kitchen for a bit and then

stops. She grabs a bag or coat and heads for the door.

Where are you going?

BETH: Out.

CHARLIE: Out...where?

BETH: I don't know. It's not like I've ever done this before. *(Pause.)* I'll be at Mom's.

CHARLIE: When will you be back?

Pause.

BETH: I don't know.

BETH exits. We hear the sounds of a car door slamming shut, and the car driving away. CHARLIE looks out the window. Music plays. CHARLIE wanders around, looking in the fridge, trying to find some ownership over this kitchen, but not really knowing what to do. Props for the next scene can be added by stage hands as CHARLIE wanders around. CHARLIE can interact with and use some of the props added (eating from take-out boxes.), to indicate that time is passing. He can tousle his hair and change his clothes. He is lost. His hair gets dirtier and his clothes may get stained. Lights and sound may be used to indicate that a week has passed. He eventually crawls under a blanket on the couch. He is not happy about sleeping on the couch, but is too proud to show discomfort. He is restless under the covers, and has trouble getting comfortable, tossing and turning and trying to get the pillow just right. Eventually, he drifts into a sleep.

Jeff Stone (Charlie)

Scene Three

There is a flow from the previous scene with no break.

It is one week later, on a Saturday morning. The sun has risen but the room is somewhat dark, as the curtains are drawn. There is evidence that the cooking and cleaning have been neglected. There are boxes of take-out meals, pizza boxes, and cans opened for a quick dinner. There are clothes and papers lying around. CHARLIE is on the couch under a blanket. MICHAEL comes in the door, using a key, in the half-light. He has a friend with him; KEVIN, and a small garbage bag full of dirty laundry. They are laughing and talking as they approach and can ad lib lines if desired as they approach and open the door. KEVIN is being giggly. MICHAEL opens the door and sees it is dark.

MICHAEL: Shhh… They might be sleeping.

KEVIN: Sorry, man.

They walk in and look around in the half light.

MICHAEL: *(Quietly.)* Holy shit. What the hell tornado hit this place?

CHARLIE stirs and moans, still asleep.

Dad?

CHARLIE: *(Still sleeping, moaning, may be unclear.)* Noooo… don't!

CHARLIE is still sleeping. MICHAEL gets closer and speaks softly.

MICHAEL: Dad?

KEVIN: Dude, let him sleep.

CHARLIE: *(Dreaming, half coherent.)* No, Mrs. Weaver…I… no…

KEVIN: What's he saying?

MICHAEL: It's OK. He does this all the time.

CHARLIE: *(Still dreaming)* I'm sorry. I forgot… *(Less coherent.)*I don't say you no do what no …

MICHAEL: *(Touching him gently.)* Dad…

KEVIN: No, don't wake him up. Let's listen.

Pause.

CHARLIE: I'll hand it in Friday! I promise! Don't call my parents!

KEVIN: Oh man, this is too funny.

MICHAEL: I better wake him up.

KEVIN: No…wait…this is a classic nightmare! I got it… watch this… *(He talks to CHARLIE slowly, moving close to him, pretending to be a female teacher.)* So… you're sorry are you, young man? Well 'sorry' isn't good enough *(Pause.)* That paper is three weeks late and I'm tired of excuses. This is high school, Master Campbell. I'm afraid there will be severe penalties, which, *(His voice becomes high, fake and sultry here.)* if you're lucky, may involve handcuffs and whipped cream, and minty-flavoured lubricants.

CHARLIE: *(Starting to wake but dazed.)* What?

MICHAEL: He's waking up.

KEVIN: Oh shit. *(He moves away from them quickly.)*

CHARLIE: Where am I?

MICHAEL: Dad, it's me.

CHARLIE: Michael?

MICHAEL: Yeah. I'm home.

CHARLIE: What's going on? Where am I?

MICHAEL: You're on the couch. Are you OK?

CHARLIE: Of course I'm OK. Why?

MICHAEL: You were dreaming.

CHARLIE: No I wasn't.

MICHAEL: Well you were talking in your sleep again.

CHARLIE: Highly unlikely.

MICHAEL: Whatever.

Pause.

CHARLIE: You're home. *(Beat.)* But you've only been gone a week.

MICHAEL: Why are you on the couch?

Pause.

CHARLIE: The…mattress hurts my back.

MICHAEL: But…

CHARLIE: Never mind. What time is it?

MICHAEL: Almost eight. Where's Mom?

CHARLIE: Eight? Are you sure?

MICHAEL: Yeah.

CHARLIE: I slept in.

MICHAEL: Where's Mom?

CHARLIE: Your mother…is not here. She is…at your Nanna's cottage…

MICHAEL: Since when?

CHARLIE: For the weekend.

MICHAEL: Why?

CHARLIE: She's just…gone, OK?

MICHAEL: Alright, I was just asking.

CHARLIE: I'm sorry. *(Pause.)* Let's turn some lights on in here. *(Getting up, he sees KEVIN.)* Oh. Hello.

KEVIN: Hello Mr. Campbell.

MICHAEL: Dad, this is my friend Kevin, from my dorm.

CHARLIE: Hello Kevin.

KEVIN: It's great to meet you, sir.

CHARLIE: It's good to meet you too. *(Pause.)* Alright then… have you two had breakfast?

MICHAEL: Yes.

KEVIN: But that was two hours ago. More of a pre-breakfast, really.

CHARLIE: How about I make us some of my gourmet blueberry waffles?

KEVIN: Sounds good to me.

MICHAEL: Since when do you make waffles?

CHARLIE: Since I woke up the other day, and realized…that I've always wanted a waffle iron. So, I went out and bought one. *(He indicates his waffle iron on the counter.)*

MICHAEL opens a cupboard and takes out a waffle iron.

Well I couldn't find it.

Pause.

KEVIN: Are the blueberries fresh?

CHARLIE: Frozen.

MICHAEL: Don't bother, Dad.

KEVIN: But…he's offering.

CHARLIE: It's no bother. Really…I think I still have some mix left from dinner last night. *(The bowl is on the counter.)*

Pause.

KEVIN: Maybe I'll just have a banana.

CHARLIE: Sure. Help yourself.

KEVIN grabs a banana from the fruit bowl and offers it to MICHAEL.

MICHAEL: Ahhh…no. Thanks.

KEVIN sees CHARLIE is cleaning.

KEVIN: Can I help?

CHARLIE: No. That's alright. *(Pause.)* So, where are you from, Kevin?

KEVIN: Oh, I'm from out east, sir. Cape Breton.

CHARLIE: Wonderful. I love the East Coast. The people… fabulous people there.

MICHAEL: Did you guys have a party here last night or something? This place is gross.

CHARLIE: We've been…busy. How did you get here anyway?

MICHAEL: We caught a ride. Should I have called and warned you or something?

CHARLIE: No. It's fine. Listen, I haven't had shower in a while…I should go make myself presentable.

MICHAEL: You're fine, Dad.

KEVIN: Let him go, Michael.

CHARLIE: No, really. I can't even stand myself. I'll be right back. Help yourselves to…whatever you can find in my absence.

CHARLIE exits.

KEVIN: I'm just gonna tidy things up a little.

MICHAEL: Knock yourself out.

KEVIN: *(Starting to clean up garbage.)* Man, that is not how I pictured your dad.

MICHAEL: I'm not sure that is my dad.

KEVIN: Do you have a garbage bag? *(Pause, MICHAEL gets him a garbage bag.)* Listen…the whole couch thing… *not* a good sign.

MICHAEL: What do you mean?

KEVIN: Your dad slept on the couch.

MICHAEL: Probably watching a game.

KEVIN: Hmmm. How long has your mom been away?

MICHAEL: What are you talking about?

KEVIN: Michael, something's wrong here.

MICHAEL: Kevin…

KEVIN: Michael…your lawn needs mowing. Your kitchen is one big…science experiment. And your dad is a complete…grunge squirrel.

MICHAEL: So…?

KEVIN: Your parents' marriage may be in trouble.

MICHAEL: No. You're way off.

KEVIN: It's everywhere, man. Parents who have been sticking it out for the sake of the kids, right? Then when they're gone, they figure there's no reason to keep staring at each other. They don't want to pretend to be happy, right…so they get a divorce.

MICHAEL: My parents have not been sticking it out—

KEVIN: Well they're not gonna *tell* you that. I told you…my parents split in the summer. They didn't even wait till I was out the door. It's an epidemic.

MICHAEL: Yeah, but not my parents.

KEVIN: That's denial, dude. It was on that psych quiz yesterday, remember?

MICHAEL: I'm not in denial.

KEVIN: You're denying that you're in denial. There's gotta be a diagnosis for that too.

Pause.

Anyway, I'll be able to deliver my verdict about your folks after I see them together.

MICHAEL: Whatever. *(Pause. MICHAEL looks in the bread cupboard.)* OK, will you quit with the cleaning, you're driving me nuts. *(At this point there should still be garbage around the kitchen. It is not clean yet.)*

KEVIN: Alright. Alright. *(Pause.)* Whatcha lookin' for?

MICHAEL: Fresh bagels.

KEVIN: Good luck finding anything fresh in this garbage dump. *(He looks in the freezer.)* You've got frozen.

MICHAEL: *(Looking in cupboards.)* I hate defrosting shit.

KEVIN: Oh yes. I concur. Fresh is best.

MICHAEL finds sugary cereal.

MICHAEL: Bingo.

KEVIN: And sugary cereal is always acceptable. *(Pause, they sit down to eat.)* So… you're gonna tell them, right?

MICHAEL: Yes, I'll tell them.

KEVIN makes chicken noises.

I said I'd do it, and I'll do it.

KEVIN: Today?

MICHAEL: Today.

KEVIN: They're gonna find out anyway.

MICHAEL: I know.

KEVIN: Is your dad gonna be pissed?

MICHAEL: I think so.

KEVIN: Your mom will be cool?

MICHAEL: She'll be more…surprised…disappointed maybe.

KEVIN: Disappointed…that's worse than pissed.

MICHAEL: Tell me about it.

KEVIN: Listen, you, ah…want me to go for a walk or something…when you talk to them?

MICHAEL: It's kind of drizzly outside.

KEVIN: Yeah. Plus, you live out in the country, so there's nowhere to go.

MICHAEL: True.

KEVIN: I could go to your bedroom and look at your porn collection.

MICHAEL: What porn collection?

KEVIN: *(Rummaging for more food.)* Confiscated?

MICHAEL: Just the good ones. And you can stay anyway. It's fine.

KEVIN: OK. *(He finds a box of cookies.)* Hey…jackpot!

MICHAEL: What's up with all this junk food? Mom never buys cookies.

KEVIN: Are they health freaks or something?

MICHAEL: I told you, remember? I was sick for a while. I had Hodgkin's disease.

KEVIN: That's…

MICHAEL: Cancer, yeah.

KEVIN: Serious shit.

MICHAEL: My mom got a little weird about preservatives and stuff.

KEVIN: Well, apparently things are different now. These cookies have *trans fat*.

MICHAEL: No way.

KEVIN: I think you only find out what your parents are really like after you leave home.

MICHAEL: Maybe.

KEVIN: When my parents split, my mom lost thirty pounds and dyed her hair purple.

MICHAEL: Really?

KEVIN: No lie. *(Seeing a family picture and picking it up.)* Hey, is that your mom?

MICHAEL: Yeah.

KEVIN: Man, your mom's hot!

MICHAEL: Put that back!

KEVIN: Nice rack!

MICHAEL: *(Shoving KEVIN.)* Shut up!

KEVIN: I'm serious. Your mom is bangin'!

MICHAEL playfully attacks KEVIN and the boys engage in a playful wrestling match, oblivious to anything else. The actors can ad lib a few lines in this section.

BETH enters and sees MICHAEL. She hangs up her keys.

BETH: Michael? Sweetheart...you're home!

MICHAEL: Hey, Mom.

BETH: I can't believe you're here!

MICHAEL: I thought Dad said you were at Nanna's cottage for the weekend.

BETH: Oh...well...I forgot something.

MICHAEL: Yeah. Mom, this is Kevin...he's a friend from my dorm.

BETH: Nice to meet you.

KEVIN: Pleased to meet *you*, Mrs. Campbell.

BETH: Oh, call me Beth, please.

Pause.

KEVIN: Beth it is.

BETH: Michael, is everything alright?

MICHAEL: Yeah.

BETH: We weren't expecting you.

MICHAEL: I felt like coming home, so we caught a ride.

BETH: That's great. And Kevin will join us for dinner?

KEVIN: I'm yours for the weekend

BETH: Good. I better pick up some food. I'm not sure what we have in the house. Do you have any favourites, Kevin? Allergies?

KEVIN: I'll eat pretty much anything.

MICHAEL: Ah…why don't we go out for dinner?

BETH: That's a good idea. This place isn't quite ready for company.

MICHAEL: I guess I should have called first.

BETH: Oh, I would guess Kevin's seen a messy kitchen before, right?

KEVIN: I've pretty much seen it all, Beth.

BETH: Is that right?

MICHAEL: We'll help you clean up.

BETH: No. You are not here to work. And this is your father's mess. We'll let him worry about it. *(Pause.)* Let's sit and chat. *(She leads them to the table or the couch area. They have to move garbage or blankets out of the way.)* So…how did that first psych quiz go yesterday?

MICHAEL: I think I did alright.

BETH: And did you get those books you needed for English?

MICHAEL: Yes.

BETH: Good. *(Pause.)* So, where are you from, Kevin?

KEVIN: Oh, I'm from out east... Cape Breton, ma'am. I mean, Beth.

BETH: Do you have family here?

KEVIN: Oh, no...they're all still back at the coast.

BETH: And what are you studying?

KEVIN: Aging and palliative care.

BETH: Interesting.

KEVIN: I'm fascinated by older people.

BETH: Oh really?

KEVIN: I'm particularly intrigued by the process of aging, and the current cultural preoccupation with the slowing down of that process. I don't understand it, really. I think mature people are quite beautiful... there's a special...sexiness in the wisdom that comes from having lived, that the young can never hope to capture.

BETH: Oh my goodness isn't that interesting...I'd enjoy hearing more about your theories on aging, Kevin.

KEVIN: It would be my pleasure...Beth.

BETH: Well, you are certainly welcome in our home any time. We love having Michael's friends here.

KEVIN: Thank you for the invitation. And may I say that you have a very nice... *(MICHAEL hits him.)* home.

BETH: Thank you.

Pause.

MICHAEL: Is everything OK, Mom?

BETH: Of course, Michael. Why?

MICHAEL: It just looks like—

CHARLIE enters.

CHARLIE: You're home.

BETH: Why don't I make some coffee? *(She gets up to make coffee. CHARLIE starts cleaning the kitchen.)*

CHARLIE: *(Sotto voce.)* Are you…home?

BETH: I don't know. Go sit with them. You can clean up later.

CHARLIE: *(Sotto voce.)* I want to clean up now. *(He starts to clean away the garbage.)*

BETH: Fine.

CHARLIE: Fine.

BETH: Fine.

MICHAEL: I brought some laundry home, Mom. Is that OK?

BETH: *(Hugging him.)* Yes, sweetheart. Of course it's OK. It's wonderful. I'm so happy to have you home. *(Pause.)* And we're going to have a party to celebrate three years. I should bake a cake!

MICHAEL: It's OK…Mom.

BETH: No, I want to. *(Pause.)* I…don't know if we have any chocolate though. You like chocolate.

MICHAEL: It doesn't have to be chocolate.

BETH: Where's your laundry? *(MICHAEL gives her the bag of laundry, she's fighting tears.)* I'll start this for you. Then I'll find some chocolate and bake you a cake and…we'll have a celebration.

BETH exits on the verge of tears. KEVIN starts to

tidy up the couch area.

MICHAEL: *(To CHARLIE.)* Is Mom OK?

CHARLIE: She'll be fine. Let's talk about you. How is school? You might be feeling a bit overwhelmed right now, with midterms just around the corner.

CHARLIE sees that KEVIN has started to tidy up the sheets.

MICHAEL: It's OK. It's—

CHARLIE: Oh, Kevin...you don't have to do that.

KEVIN: I don't mind. I like a tidy environment. At home this was one of my regular chores. *(Pause.)* How's your back?

CHARLIE: My back is fine. Why?

KEVIN: No reason. Where do you want this stuff?

CHARLIE: I'll take it.

He throws it in a corner. BETH enters.

BETH: Alright...cake. *(BETH starts to gather the ingredients for a cake.)* So, how is dorm life going for you two?

KEVIN: It's great, never boring.

MICHAEL: It's hard to sleep sometimes.

KEVIN: The thing is...Beth...that...girls are really noisy. Don't you agree? I mean, I know you're a girl yourself and everything, but, really...I don't have sisters and I had no idea that they were so noisy. Mr. Campbell, do you think girls are noisier than guys?

Pause.

CHARLIE: No comment.

MICHAEL: But Kevin and I have discovered this place that the girls don't know about yet, so when we want quiet we go there to study.

KEVIN: *(There's a private joke here.)* Yeah, we study there a lot.

BETH: That's wonderful.

KEVIN pulls MICHAEL aside.

MICHAEL: What?

KEVIN: Do it.

MICHAEL: Now?

KEVIN: Yes.

MICHAEL: Alright. *(Pause.)* Um…Mom, Dad…can I talk to you about something for a minute?

BETH: Sure, sweetheart. What is it?

MICHAEL: Can we sit down?

BETH: Alright.

They all sit at the kitchen table. KEVIN sits too, and the others look at him. He gets up.

KEVIN: I'll just give you guys some space. How 'bout I go for a walk outside? *(He opens the door.)* Except it's kinda raining…so how 'bout I just sit over here and listen to my music? *(He moves to the couch area and puts on some headphones, but is listening to their conversation.)*

BETH: Is everything alright?

MICHAEL: There's something I need to tell you.

BETH: You sound serious.

MICHAEL: I guess it sort of is…but not, like, really serious.

BETH: Are you feeling alright?

MICHAEL: Mom…yes. This is not about my health. I feel great. So, OK, this is it…I've been thinking a lot lately, and…I've sort of discovered…something important…about myself.

CHARLIE: Go on…

MICHAEL: I've been thinking about this for a while, and I wasn't sure, so I didn't tell you. Now, I'm very sure. So this is it…I'm…

BETH: Anything you *are* is perfectly OK with us, Michael.

CHARLIE: Son, we love you no matter what your…sexual preferences might be.

MICHAEL: No! Mom… Dad…no. Shit. I'm not…gay.

BETH: You're not?

MICHAEL: No!

CHARLIE: Oh.

KEVIN: Oh he's definitely not gay. It's probably my fault, the whole misunderstanding… I give off an androgynous vibe sometimes, so, you may have thought that Michael and I…

MICHAEL: Kevin…headphones! *(Pause.)* Mom, Dad, listen… it's about…school.

CHARLIE: School?

MICHAEL: Yeah. The whole engineering thing.

CHARLIE: You're finding it difficult?

MICHAEL: No…it's not that.

CHARLIE: I know how hard that program is, Michael. I had

the same trepidations when I started engineering.

MICHAEL: Yeah, and you quit.

CHARLIE: No…I switched programs.

MICHAEL: OK…and you're glad you did, right?

CHARLIE: Yes, but—

BETH: You want to quit school?

MICHAEL: I mean…now you're a psychologist and you're happy, right?

CHARLIE: Yes, Michael. But this is about you, not me. If you need a tutor, we'll get you one.

MICHAEL: Dad…it's not… *(Pause.)* The thing is… I don't want to be an engineer any more.

CHARLIE: What?!

BETH: Michael? What do you mean?

MICHAEL: I thought I wanted it; when I applied and everything…but then this summer I realized that just because I was good at something doesn't mean that I have to do it for a job.

CHARLIE: Engineering isn't a job, son…it's a career.

BETH: You're not listening to him, Charlie. It's not what he wants.

CHARLIE: Nobody knows what they want at eighteen. But you can't just flop around and change your mind at the drop of a hat. He just started! This will open doors for him.

MICHAEL: Dad, I—

CHARLIE: You're not quitting.

BETH: Charlie!

MICHAEL: Shit! I knew this would happen! How come for you it's 'switching programs' and for me it's quitting?

CHARLIE: Now wait just a minute...

BETH: Charlie, listen to him. Michael, what is it you want to do?

Pause.

MICHAEL: I want to be a nurse.

CHARLIE: A nurse? And...you're...not—

BETH: Charlie! *(Beat.)* Sweetheart...you want to be a nurse.

MICHAEL: It's...this is gonna sound stupid, but...it's like a calling, you know? I've spent so much time in hospitals for what feels like my whole life, and it feels like a kind of...home. It feels right to me. It's what I want to do...to heal people. I might be more interested in psychology even; like you, Dad. I'm not sure.

CHARLIE: You're not sure?

MICHAEL: I know that I want to work in a hospital, with people, not drawings and numbers.

BETH: Michael...that's wonderful.

KEVIN: He's going to be an amazing nurse, Mr. and Mrs. Campbell. He's strong, and gentle...but as several females could attest...not gay.

MICHAEL: Thank you, Kevin.

BETH: That's beautiful, sweetheart.

MICHAEL: I don't even have to switch schools. U. of T. has a nursing program. I've talked to the dean and I can switch right now.

BETH: Why didn't you tell us in the summer?

MICHAEL: I don't know. It seemed so important to you.

BETH: *(To CHARLIE.)* To you. He didn't want to disappoint—

CHARLIE: Beth, I don't think…

BETH and CHARLIE talk over each other here and for perhaps the first time are arguing in front of MICHAEL.

BETH: …his father. I told you there was too much pressure on him. He obviously just wanted to…

CHARLIE: All I did was encourage him to follow his skills. The engineering program is one of the…

BETH: No. You tried to make him live out your father's agenda…

CHARLIE: He's got the chance to—

BETH: He doesn't want to be an engineer. And you didn't either.

CHARLIE: I failed, Beth. I failed because it was too hard, but he can do it. I know he can…

BETH: You think you failed? Is that what you think? Those are your father's words, Charlie. The only thing you failed at was not telling him what you really wanted. You didn't want to be an engineer any more than Michael does. *(Pause.)* Your father is the one who failed. He failed you! And you're still trying to win his approval, through your son…and for what?

CHARLIE: I'm trying to support my son.

BETH: There's supporting and there's pushing. You don't listen to him.

CHARLIE: How was I supposed to know he didn't want it? I asked him

BETH: It's between the lines, Charlie. If we had just listened to what he wasn't saying...

CHARLIE: What he wasn't saying? I'm supposed to know what he wasn't saying?

BETH: You know what I mean.

CHARLIE: No, I don't.

Pause.

BETH: I can't breathe. Is it hot in here?

KEVIN: You may be experiencing one of the classic symptoms of perimenopause, Beth.

BETH: No Kevin, it's not a hot flash.

KEVIN: Just trying to help.

BETH: It's alright. I like that you say what's on your mind. That's what I want for this family. I want us to be able to tell each other things, even if it's hard. I don't want secrets. *(She runs from the room.)*

Long awkward pause.

KEVIN: Awkward...

MICHAEL: What was Mom talking about?

CHARLIE: Your mother and I are...going through a difficult period right now.

MICHAEL: Dad, just tell me what's happening.

CHARLIE: I think we better talk. *(Pause.)* Kevin, Michael and I have some important family business to discuss. If you don't mind...could you...?

KEVIN: Oh...sure. I'll get outa here. But...could I just have *two seconds* with my man here first?

Pause.

CHARLIE: Sure. I need some fresh air anyway.

CHARLIE exits outside.

KEVIN: Does he know it's raining out there?

MICHAEL: What's up?

KEVIN: Michael, your parents are obviously in deep trouble, and I think it's time for a drastic measure.

MICHAEL: Kev, listen—

KEVIN: I think that we should sit them down, tell them that we love them very much, that there's nothing we wouldn't do for them, but that it's time for them both to face a few things about how their behaviours are affecting the people they love.

MICHAEL: Kevin, listen, I get what you're doing, but... interventions are for alcohol and drug addicts.

KEVIN: But why not troubled marriages? I ask you.

CHARLIE enters. He is very wet.

MICHAEL: You watch way too much reality TV. Look, right now I really need to be alone with my family. I'm sorry, but...can you just give us a minute?

KEVIN: Oh. Of course.

CHARLIE: It's raining.

KEVIN: Could I borrow an umbrella?

MICHAEL: Sure. *(MICHAEL hands him an umbrella. He gives CHARLIE a towel.)*

KEVIN: Thank you. Maybe a raincoat?

CHARLIE: Aren't you from the East Coast?

KEVIN: Yes, and over there we use a lot of umbrellas and raincoats.

MICHAEL hands KEVIN a raincoat.

MICHAEL: I'll come get you when we're done.

KEVIN: *(Embracing CHARLIE.)* Good luck Mr. Campbell.

CHARLIE: Alright, Kevin.

KEVIN exits.

Please sit down, Michael.

MICHAEL sits at the couch area.

MICHAEL: I know you're pissed but—

CHARLIE: No…no, I'm not. I overreacted.

MICHAEL: So, you'll let me quit?

CHARLIE: Pursuing a career you are passionate about is not quitting.

MICHAEL: Well if you agree with Mom, why were you guys fighting?

CHARLIE: Michael, this…tension…is not your fault. Your mother and I are both very happy that you have been honest with us, and yourself.

MICHAEL: Then what's going on?

Pause.

CHARLIE: Your mother is upset because I told her something a few weeks ago…something that I had kept a secret from her.

MICHAEL: OK…

CHARLIE: And I will tell you now, because it must be quite evident to you that something is going on, and I don't want you to be confused.

MICHAEL: Alright…

CHARLIE: Michael, I had a growth removed from my scrotum in July. They're doing tests to determine whether it's—

MICHAEL: Cancer.

CHARLIE: No…I mean…yes. They know it *was*…but they need to find out if it's spread, so things are a bit tense as we wait for the news.

MICHAEL: You have cancer?

CHARLIE: *Had*… I feel confident we can speak of it in the past tense.

MICHAEL: OK. What numbers did they give you?

CHARLIE: We'll know more on the twenty-fifth of this month.

MICHAEL: OK. *(Pause.)* Well, that completely sucks.

CHARLIE: It'll be fine.

MICHAEL: *(Hugs his father.)* I'm sorry, Dad.

CHARLIE: I know.

MICHAEL: How do you feel?

CHARLIE: I feel good.

Pause.

MICHAEL: OK. But I don't get it. Why are you and Mom fighting?

CHARLIE: It's complicated.

MICHAEL: You're sick…it doesn't make sense.

CHARLIE: I'm not sick. I feel fine.

MICHAEL: OK…you're not sick. You just have cancer, that's all…

CHARLIE: *Had…*

MICHAEL: Whatever. You don't know that. But why is Mom crying?

CHARLIE: Your mother is upset that I didn't tell her about it right away.

MICHAEL: Oh. Yeah, I can see that.

CHARLIE: We're just…taking a bit of space for ourselves for now.

MICHAEL: What?…you're…what? What does that mean?

CHARLIE: I'm not sure right now.

MICHAEL: Did Mom move out?

CHARLIE: No long-term decisions have been—

MICHAEL: Are you getting a divorce?

Pause.

CHARLIE: I have no plans to divorce your mother.

MICHAEL: So does Mom want a divorce?

CHARLIE: I don't know what she wants right now.

MICHAEL: Well, just…find out…OK?…and then…whatever it is she wants you to do, just do it, alright?

CHARLIE: It's not that simple, Michael. A lot has happened—

MICHAEL: What? What's happened? You've been happy together, haven't you?

CHARLIE: Yes, but…

MICHAEL: I need Mom. MOM! Can you come in here?

CHARLIE: It might be best to leave it alone for now.

MICHAEL: No. I want to know. MOM!!

BETH enters.

BETH: What is it? What's wrong?

MICHAEL: Will you tell me what's going on?

BETH: What do you mean?

MICHAEL: Oh come on…just stop lying, both of you. I come in and find Dad sleeping on the couch…and Mom's not even living here any more! You guys can't even be in the same room together… *(To BETH.)* You're crying at every little thing…this place looks like a friggin' frat house…and you yelled at each other… even Kevin could tell something was wrong.

BETH: I think your father has something to tell you.

CHARLIE: I already told him.

BETH: You told him?

CHARLIE: Yes.

MICHAEL: What…the cancer thing? Yeah, he told me.

BETH: You're alright?

MICHAEL: Yeah… I mean, no, of course not, but—

BETH: Is that all you told him?

CHARLIE: No…

MICHAEL: Why are you fighting?

BETH: Sweetheart, this is between your father and I.

MICHAEL: But it feels weird.

CHARLIE: It's for us to work out.

MICHAEL: So then you're working it out?

Pause.

Are you divorcing dad?

BETH: *(To CHARLIE.)* Did you tell him that?

CHARLIE: I didn't know what to tell him, Beth.

BETH: Why would you...? Michael, your dad and I are struggling with some issues right now, but—

MICHAEL: You're getting a divorce, aren't you?

BETH: We haven't discussed it.

MICHAEL: Well can you tell me for sure that you're not?

Pause. Silence.

No way. This is...

CHARLIE: Son, it's...

MICHAEL: Bullshit!

BETH: Michael!

CHARLIE: It's not about you.

MICHAEL: Bullshit!

BETH: What your dad means is that whatever happens between us, you'll always have us both. All our love.

MICHAEL: Like that's supposed to make me feel better? Mom...he's sick. How can you...?

BETH: Michael, this is about far more than what's happening with your dad's health right now.

MICHAEL: OK, so, have you always been unhappy? Was I, like, completely fooled? Were you waiting for me to leave so you could split?

CHARLIE: No.

BETH: No!

CHARLIE: Of course not.

MICHAEL: Is somebody having an affair?

CHARLIE: No! Beth…

BETH: No!

CHARLIE & BETH: No.

MICHAEL: So it's nothing horrible then, right? Nothing that can't be fixed?

BETH: It's nothing horrible, no.

MICHAEL: Then just…fix it, OK. Because…you'd look really stupid with purple hair, Mom.

BETH: What?

MICHAEL: Nothing.

CHARLIE: You need to focus on your schoolwork and let your mother and I—

MICHAEL: What? You think I can focus on school when I don't even know if I have a family anymore?

BETH: We'll always be your family. Even if—

MICHAEL: You think that if you get a divorce, that it shouldn't affect me?

BETH: Of course not—

MICHAEL: Because I'm eighteen and I'm supposed to be old enough to understand…whatever it is I'm supposed to understand.

BETH: Sweetheart—

MICHAEL: Well I don't understand it.

CHARLIE: Michael—

MICHAEL: Not any of it.

BETH: Michael—

MICHAEL: You want to know what's going through my head right now? I'm thinking about every moment in my entire life that I thought was really happy…and I'm wondering if it was all a big lie. If it was all just a pile of—

BETH: No.

MICHAEL: Bullshit.

BETH: Michael, please don't.

CHARLIE: Let him be angry.

Pause.

MICHAEL: I get it. It's because I was sick, right?

BETH: What?

MICHAEL: Like maybe my cancer was the reason you stayed together. For your poor sick son, right?

BETH: No.

MICHAEL: Like it's not worth the effort unless somebody's dying? Well now Dad's dying, so there you go.

CHARLIE: Michael…

MICHAEL: I wish it was me again! I wish it was me instead of you!

BETH: Charlie…?

CHARLIE: Michael, no!

BETH: You don't mean that.

MICHAEL: I do mean it! *(Pause.)* I don't want to lose this family. Not any part of it. *(Pause.)* Shit. I gotta get outa here.

BETH: Michael, don't go.

MICHAEL leaves and after a pause, BETH starts to follow.

CHARLIE: Let him be, Beth.

BETH: He needs me right now!

CHARLIE: What he needs is space. Stop smothering him.

BETH: Smothering him? I need to—

CHARLIE: He's just angry. He's had a shock, and he needs time to think. You run to him so easily.

BETH: I've got to go. *(BETH starts to leave.)*.

CHARLIE: Go on then. Go and take care of him, like you always do. Everything comes before this marriage. We'll save the whole goddamn world and just let our marriage die…

BETH: Now who's being melodramatic? *(BETH is leaving.)*

CHARLIE: Don't go out that door. *(BETH exits without a coat.)* Damn it!

Pause. We see CHARLIE alone in the space for a few minutes.

BETH enters. She is very wet.

BETH: It's raining.

CHARLIE gets her a towel.

Thank you.

Pause.

CHARLIE: Is Michael OK?

BETH: Oh, he's perfectly happy with Kevin and their stash of porn in the shed. It seems to be a cure-all. Remember we used to find that stuff everywhere. How is it we thought he was gay?

CHARLIE: Well the conversation did seem to be… *(Pause.)* You should get out of those wet clothes.

BETH: I've got to bake that cake. *(BETH starts looking in a cupboard.)* Will you help me find the chocolate?

CHARLIE: Beth…

BETH: It's supposed to be right here. *(Pause.)* Damnit! Charlie, I can't find the chocolate!

CHARLIE: I'll help you.

Pause. BETH is crying. CHARLIE approaches her gently.

Beth?

BETH: He doesn't need me anymore Charlie! I went out there and I—

CHARLIE: Oh…sweetheart…

BETH: Charlie.

BETH's legs give way and she collapses into CHARLIE's arms. CHARLIE holds her as they slide down to the floor.

CHARLIE: I've got you.

Pause.

BETH: I've been replaced…by porn.

Pause.

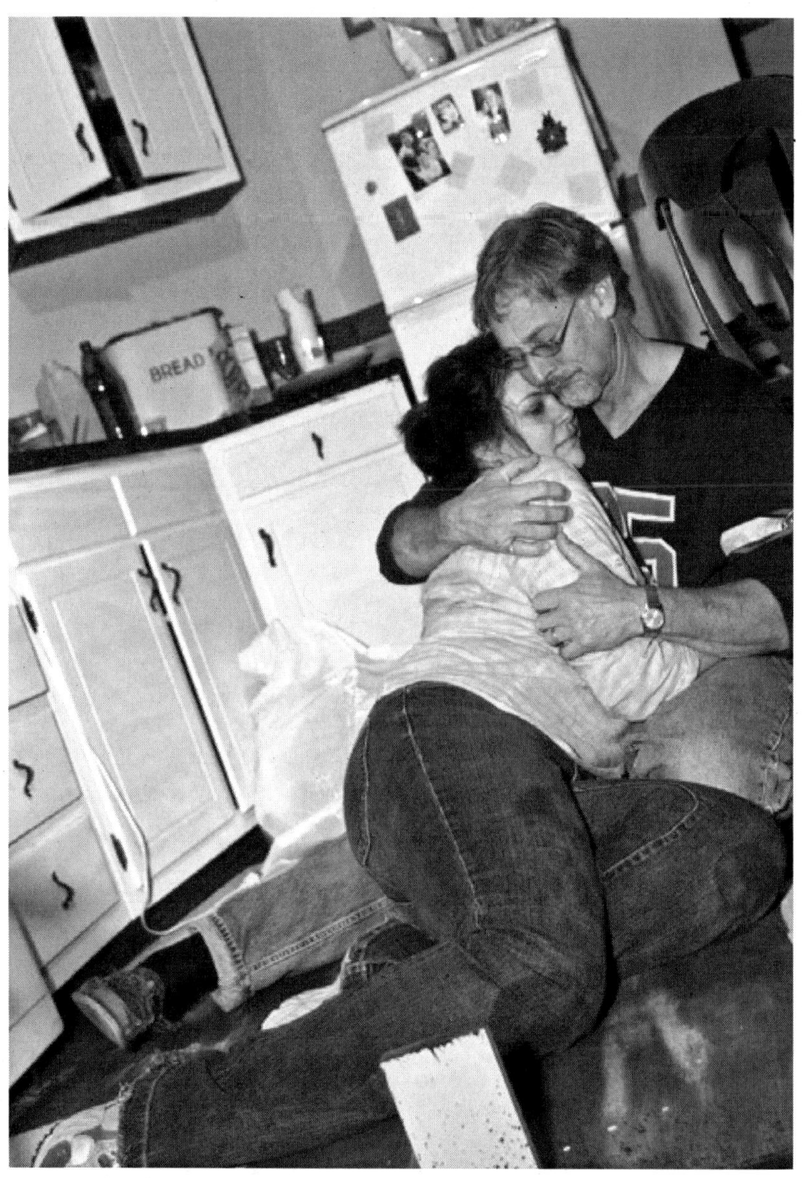

(l to r): Meredith Mills (Beth) and Jeff Stone (Charlie).

CHARLIE: No. You haven't. You couldn't be. Beth...listen to me. Michael is alive because of you, and he will always need you. *(Pause.)* And I need you too.

BETH: You do?

CHARLIE: All my stupid ranting about wanting to be in charge... *(Pause.)* The truth is... *(Pause. This is very hard for him to say.)* I don't know what to do. I don't know how to fix this...or us. *(Pause.)* I feel like such a failure. *(Pause.)* I'm sorry.

BETH: When are you going to stop expecting yourself to know everything?

Pause.

Charlie...

CHARLIE: Yes?

BETH: I have a question.

CHARLIE: OK.

BETH: Which one did they take?

CHARLIE: Which...what?

BETH: You haven't let me...see you. Was it...Curly or Moe?

Pause.

CHARLIE: It was Moe.

BETH: They took my Moe?

CHARLIE: Beth, that routine was stale. Vaudeville's dead, it has been for years.

BETH: But not the classics...Moe made me laugh.

CHARLIE: Well I'll do my best to keep you amused with the

sight of my nakedness. It's actually funnier without him. I'm all…lopsided. *(Pause.)* I'll show you.

Pause.

BETH: Charlie…

CHARLIE: Yes?

BETH: I'm scared.

CHARLIE: Me too.

Pause.

BETH: Charlie…

CHARLIE: Yes?

BETH: Maybe we can be scared together.

The End.